Copyright © 2017 Dea Bernadette D. Suselo
All rights reserved.

ISBN-13: 978-1544764511
ISBN-10: 1544764510

www.facebook.com/DeaBernadette

Thailand

Thailand

Spain

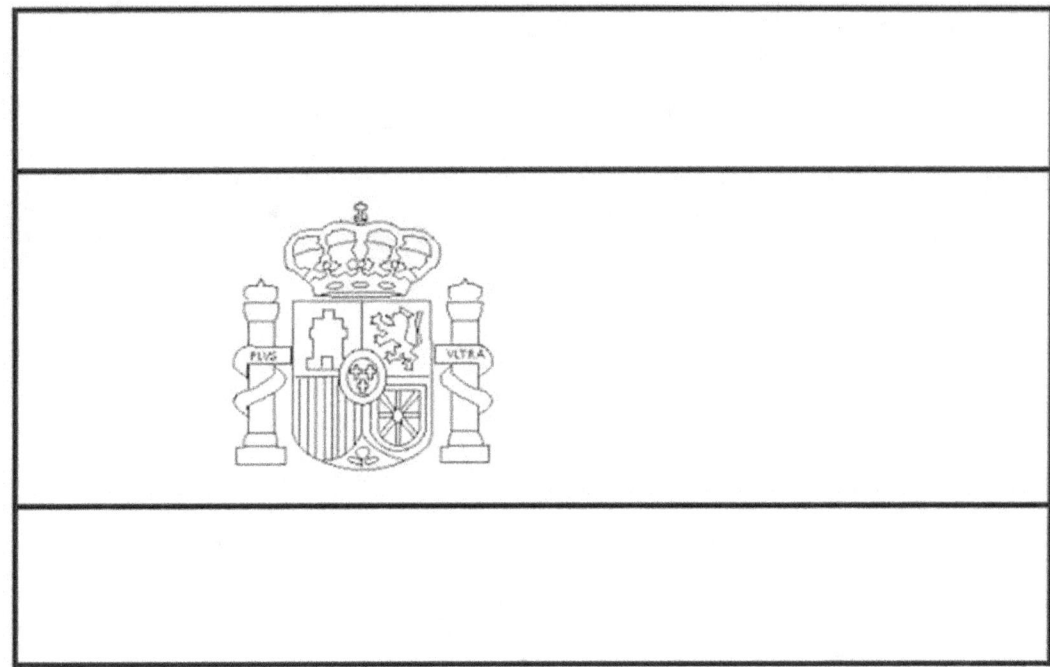

Spain

Russia

Russia

Scotland

Poland

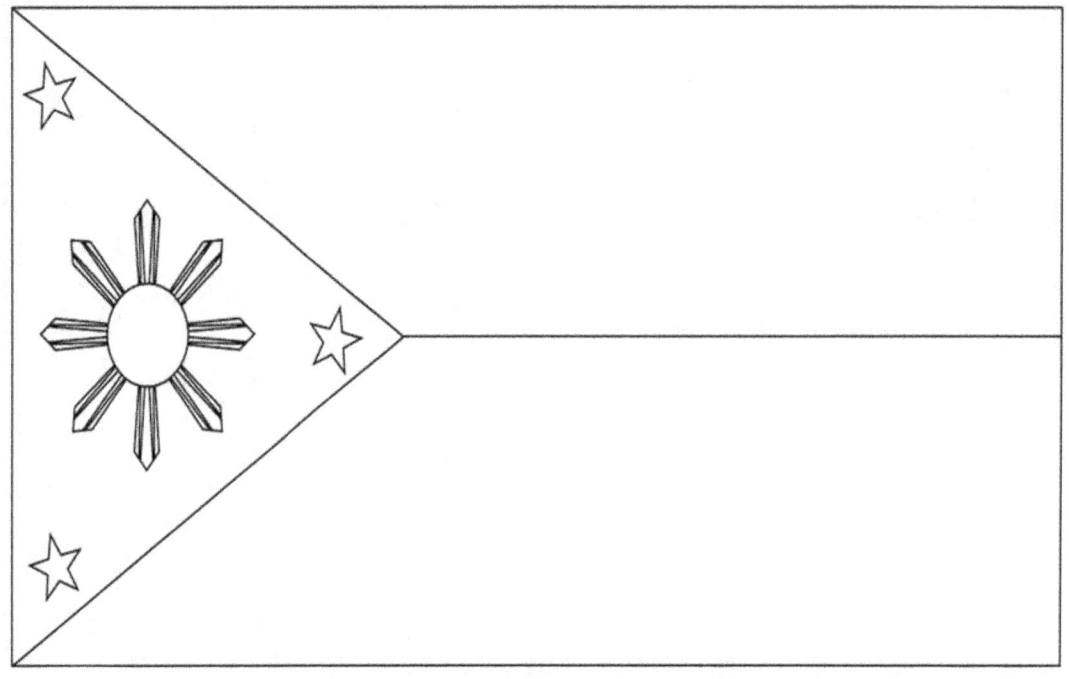

Philippines

Philippines

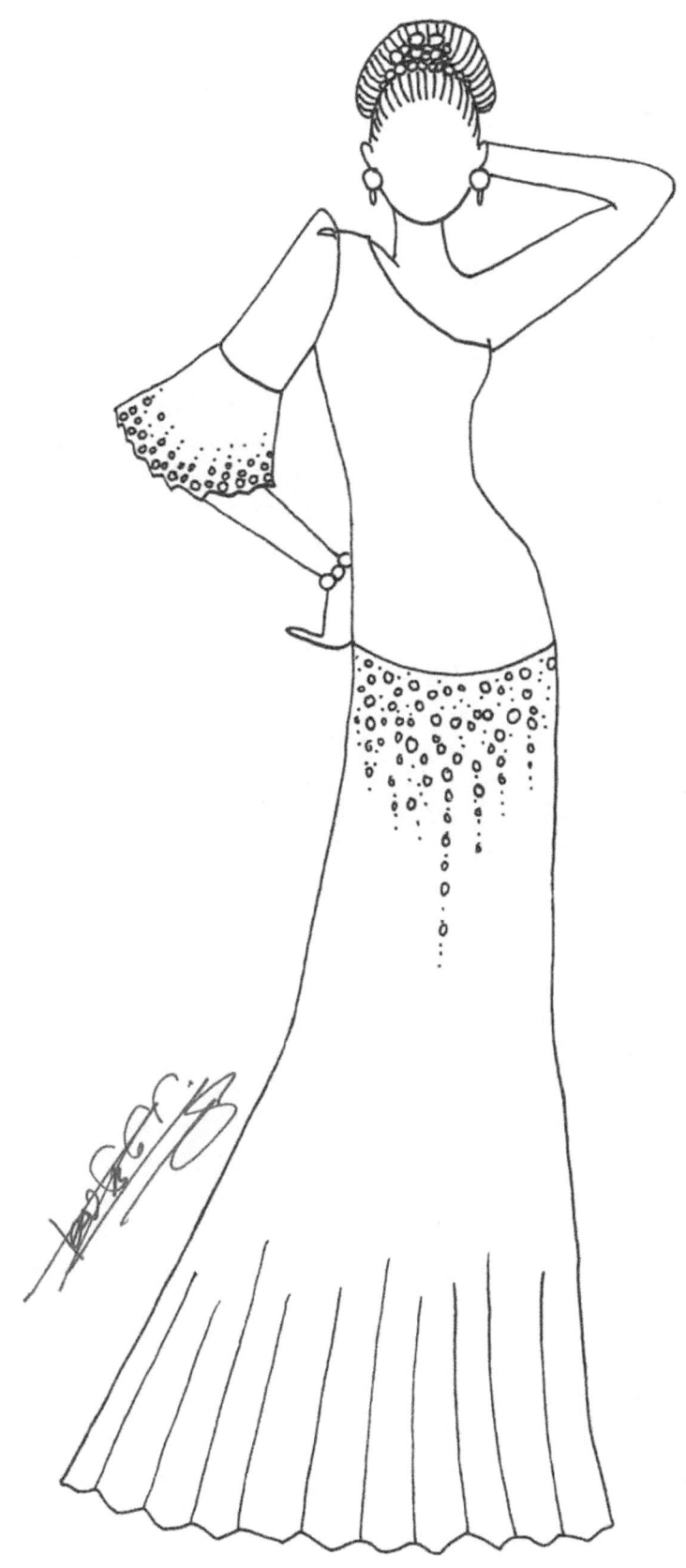

Norway

Mongolia

South Korea

South Korea

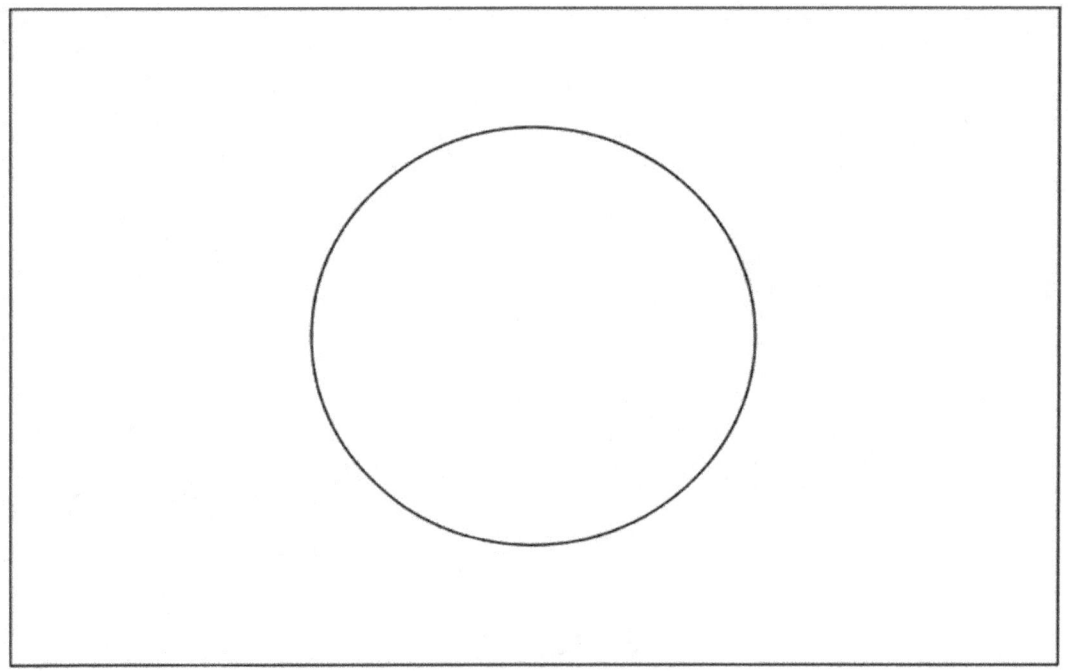

Japan

Japan

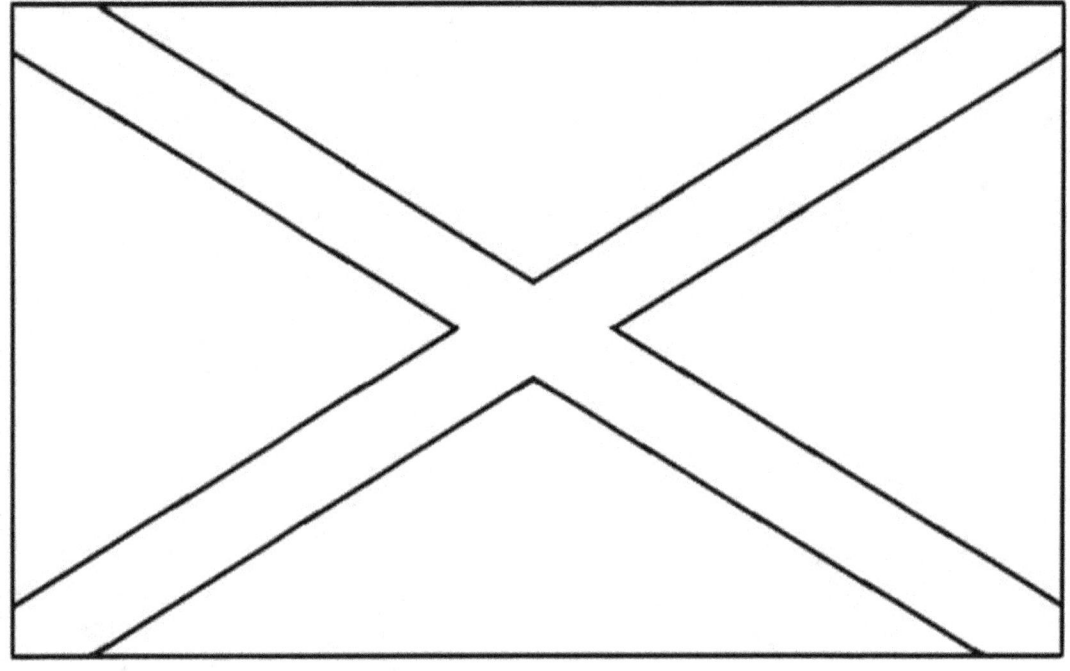

Jamaica

Indonesia

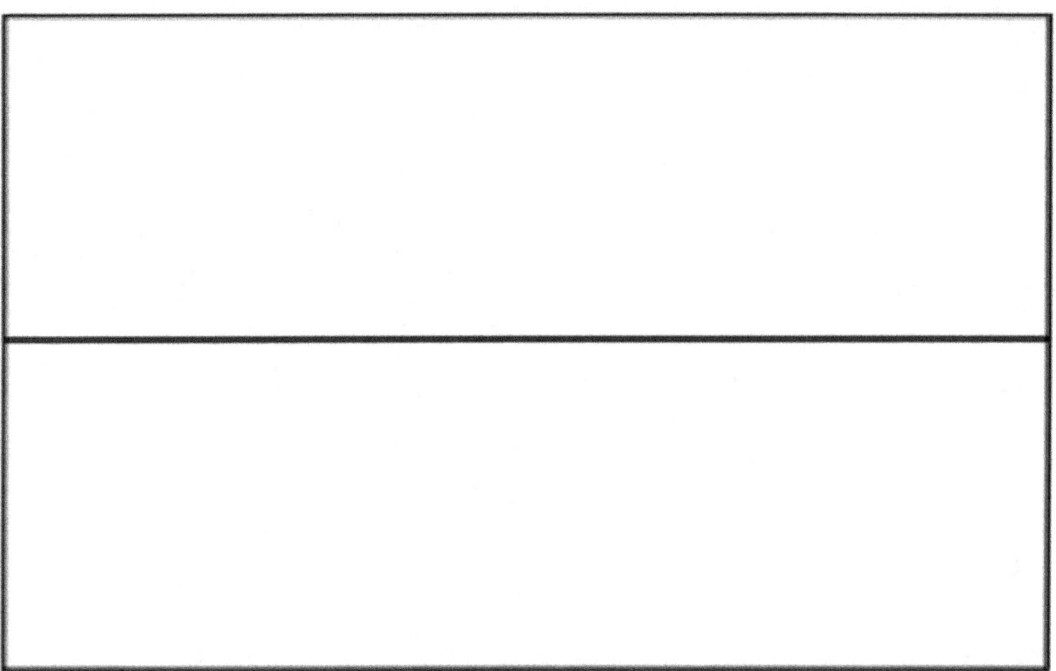

Indonesia

India

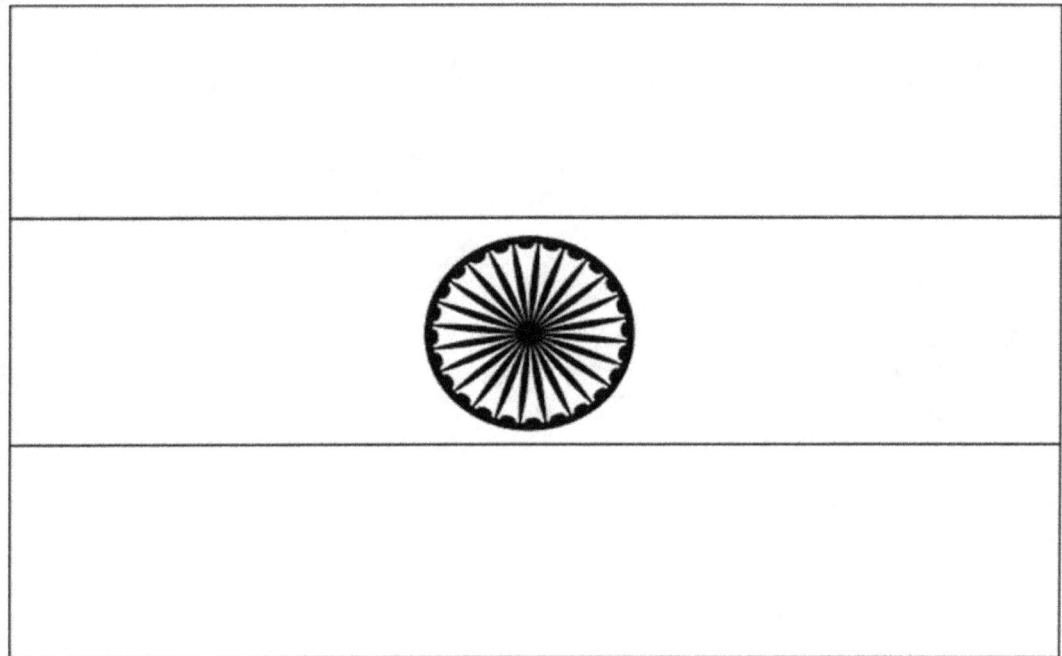

India

Greece

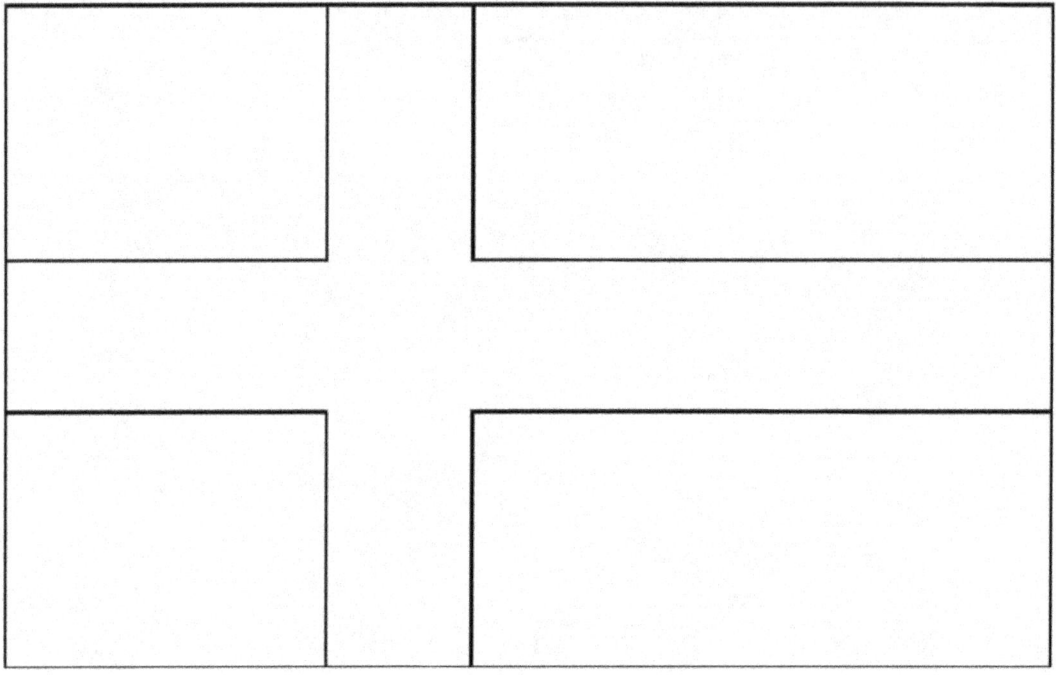

Finland

China

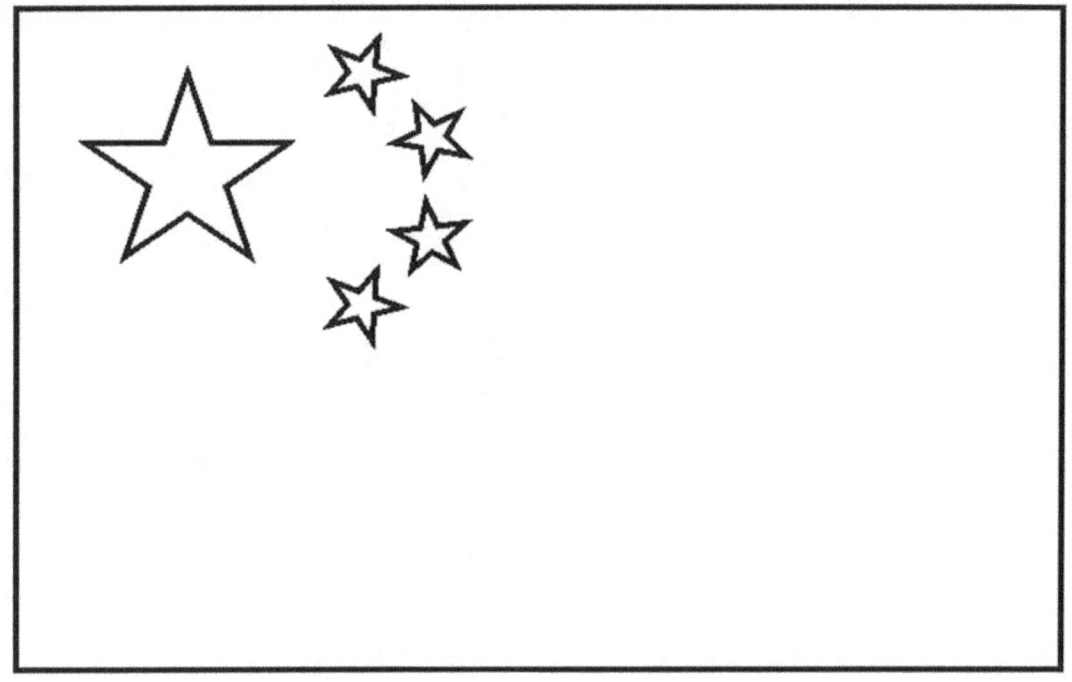

China

Cambodia

Brazil

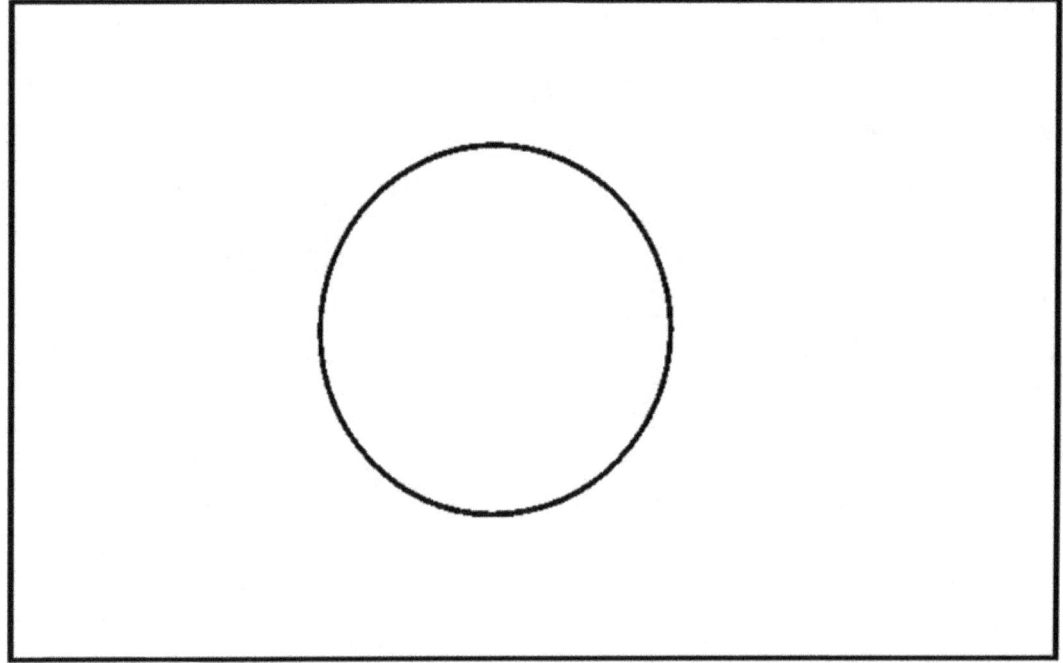

Bangladesh

Vietnam

www.ingramcontent.com/pod-product-compliance
Lightning Source LLC
Chambersburg PA
CBHW081113180526
45170CB00008B/2832